THIS HOUSE, MY BONES

Ellen

*Welcome
to my
house*

Poems

ELMAZ ABINADER

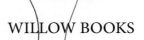

WILLOW BOOKS

Detroit, Michigan

THIS HOUSE, MY BONES

Editor: Randall Horton
Cover art: "We Shall Remain" by Manal Deeb
Author photo: Nancy Rothstein

ISBN 978-0-9897357-6-6
LCCN 2014950770

Editor's Choice Series

Willow Books, a Division of Aquarius Press
PO Box 23096
Detroit, MI 48223
www.WillowLit.net

Printed in the United States of America

Dedicated to Anthony N. Byers

and

In Memory of Robert E. Lazo

a fine heart

1964-2005

CONTENTS

ACKNOWLEDGMENTS

After Breakfast, Climb Up and Over, Arsenal, Sukoon Magazine, Fall 2014

Line of Demarcation, Heartwood, Ash Wednesday, and *In The Throat I.,* {Ex} tinguished & {Ex}tinct: An Anthology of Things That No Longer {Ex} ist, ed. John McCarthy, Twelve Winters Press 2014

Coming Clean, Kweli Journal, *Spring 2013*

The Proper Purgation, Al-Mutanabbi Street Starts Here, ed. Beau Beausoleil and Deema Shehabi, PM Press, 2012

This House, My Bones, Inclined to Speak: An Anthology of Contemporary Arab American Poetry, ed. Hayan Charara, The University of Arkansas Press, 2008

This House, My Bones, Language for a New Century, ed. by Tina Chang, Nathalie Handal, Ravi Shankar, WW Norton & Co, 2008

The Point We Meet, Come Together Imagine Peace, ed. Ann Smith, Larry Smith & Philip Metres, Bottom Dog Press, 2008

Shouldering the Sky, We Begin Here: Poems for Palestine and Lebanon, ed. Kathy Engel and Sharif Elmusa, Interlink Publishing, 2007

Many hands touched these poems, many ears heard them, many pencils scratched notes, many voices supported them with love; not to mention coffee from baristas all over the Bay Area. Elmaz writes with the power of the VONA/Voices community: the faculty, the writers, and especially board colleagues: Junot Díaz, M. Evelina Galang, Diem Jones and David Mura. On the poetry foreground: Chris Abani, Ruth Forman, Suheir Hammad, and Willie Perdomo. Steady company from Sara Campos, Faith Adiele, Yosmay del Mazo, Lenore Rebecca Harris, and Julie Skoler, keeping me tied to the chair. Residencies at Château de Lavigny in Switzerland (Ledig-Rowohlt Foundation), El Gouna Writers Residency in Egypt, Can Serrat Centro de Actividades Artisticas in Spain, MacDowell Colony, Villa Montalvo Arts

Residency, and the National Park Service South Rim of the Grand Canyon Residency. Much support from various faculty development grants via Mills College and the Meg Quigley Summer Fellowship (Women's Studies) and Faculty Development Grants from Mills College, and support from impressive colleagues at Mills—ups for Cynthia Scheinberg and Tonianne Nemeth. For holding me up in many ways: Selma Abinader, Geralyn Abinader, Jean AbiNader, and Roger AbiNader, Marlene Rubain, Maha El Said, Dalia Baissouny, Tony Khalife, Deema Shehabi, Morgan Cooper (PWW). Seni Seneviratne, Aimee Allison, Lauren Hendler, Donna Wolf, Matthew Elias. Manal Deeb's art and generosity are boundless. Anthony for heart holding; Brewster for the greatest fun. To my father, who will be 104 at the time of publication. In the memory of my brother, Elias Abi-Nader 1941-2013.

I. LINES OF DEMARCATION

I am bombarded yet   I stand
Adrienne Rich, *Planetarium*

AFTER ALEXANDER FERNANDEZ, ARCHITECT

Alejandro says truth is immediate if you rest
a sketch book on your lap and make a line

drawing without direction loosens hinges
undoes beginnings and endings

size and form   and everything
is petal or fern, its own infinity

Witness a drawing's wisdom—kindle
what must be rendered or left behind. Collect
geography on the distal phalanx, rub it over your lips

to speak not of permanence but of fluidity—
inhabitation composts a new geology

2

Wind is the pen   sea the chisel: granite, slate
striated elders' eyelids long   cliff inscribed
benedictions washed into their faces—

even the mountains burst through the earth
volcanic explosions   calm to sea…
wait, another battering comes from the wind
north and south, unkindness moves

into confusion: a murder of skin
a flattening of the head, the curve of shoulder
an anatomy carved by desires
terrain re-formed

animals show up dead   misguided after years
of knowing their own place and people
of traveling along the prescribed and certain routes
of hieroglyphs, paw prints, oases dried (en)danger ahead.

3

Anticipate the crush, the metal deposition
of this earth, the rumbling, the lifting up
sod under the hooves of the elk moose pronghorns—
the bellowing song surfacing cylindrical drums
rolling down to the river and floating

Snow fragments the larger elements:
chimney through roof, trunk extending
below branches; bark more pronounced
brick more emphatic, supple.

Boot prints carve the pure field
leading not to the house but deeper
into the wood more confounded
by the wisdom of silence.

The storm goes on:
inside the chest, catapulting
particles that have been secured
sweetly now unearthed.

4

I'll ride the tectonic landmass   visit the lost ones
speak their language   borrow their breath
sign their names to books read unread

The absence of color is where my body
touches space   where I carve from the sky
an outline of my posture planted
my position   moving headlong

I peel the skin   shave the crust away
leave membrane   bones unconstructed.

Bring the quiet of the night into the day
a map   of days, of years, of ages
          so many things

5

Footprints numberline the path   wash of tide
the shore anticipates the   sea comes toward it
casts a story   a chalk line filled with mercury memory

arrowhead rain slams glass or so I think
this storm is a dream or the insistence
of epochs entering my sleep so   I waken worrying

I have lived under the house
just off the stone road
where soldiers stripped pictures
from the wall, spray painted
limestone slurs against

the vacant residents underdressed
hovered in strange territories, felt
their bodies to find familiarity
hot whispers   a language unrecognized

6

She joined him as many do, traded lineage
for frontier, for children born away from situ
and sacrament. Dirt hard on the shoe
soles cracked to western sun   no one said life
might be alone   this is her midnight

She becomes hardwood planted in a slosh of soil
not able to hold the weight of her tide. Not native here
or anywhere. When the children are born
tendrils braid into new systems.

Reverse the stroke, comfort the hand that soothed,
un-grip the fist to make a leaf, veins like string,
soften trees to skin, of check, of chin, of heel.

Give timbre to the voices, silken the threads knitted
into the nest among the twigs. She hums a lullaby,
not for sleep or silence   memory

sprouting from an unseen root   too deep
in the soil to identify. She stays where she is left
lacing vines of ache hunger

7

Life in order is captive,
susceptible to systems. Slivers of madness
are fitted between air and object,
artery and blood.

The storm is the windfall
of grace sufficient to explain
the anxiety of our own selves as strangers
to this landscape.

So every day the power to transform
relies upon time and erosions,
storms and fires, imminent transfusion

earth's blood altered, channeling the story
that was west, east, the nothing to the
something left to translate and remember—

puzzle a cartography, locate the pieces
of tundra, of desert, palm and alder,
scaffolding encounters and desires
read that moment like no other.

8

This trumpet this timpani beats
into the inner core, injects a warmth
in the dead of an isolated winter.
Not only as explanation
for the mountains but witness to them.
We cannot stop the eruptions, each chord
incandescent/dissonant.

This may be the revelation
we wait for: that everything we
want to know, remember, treasure
holds up in our fingers—hungry for recognition:
Uncurl the fist, hold the pencil
put memory to the task.

It will skate away from you unbound
paper boat on water, particle of flower
airborne. What escapes is written elsewhere.

HEARTWOOD

(As a tree grows, older xylem cells in the center of the tree become inactive and die, forming heartwood. Because it is filled with stored sugar, dyes and oils, the heartwood is usually darker than the sapwood. The main function of the heartwood is to support the tree.)

While you watch   you are being watched
and every word you write   is scribed on arm   henna
petrified with the veins of your witnessing.

You need to grow harder than fresh limbs
slick and sentient reaching and waiting.
Solidify the cambium harden your bark
capture your tears inside your trunk
molten tributaries moving with life—

What is seen are grandmothers
skimming barbed-wire
stuffing groceries under their skirts   scrambling over the gate
as you tick off one after another up and over   your jeep idles near the wall

The pinch of the wire just refreshes old scars
they don't think as much of it as you do when

your organs soak with sugars
all the blood is trapped below
your heart. Even while it chokes you

the cells confine the color
drained from your face
as you watched them escape
to the other side of the same square of dust,   crippled tired
pulling on a power of healed-over wounds as thick as branches.

Examine those albino eyes
expressionless stupefyingly blind
and see in them rings of endless years

of stunted growth, roots lengthening below the terrain.

Where the heartwood thickens,   they have power
no one can see into the tree
where everything dead gathers and protects them
        stone core wood heart.

We don't need thunder, might, or the conversion of galaxies to withstand—
if anything we are armed with fists, conscience, rocks, history, and backs like hemp

Warfare drives us into an insistent fog, cold and frequent, a churning in the belly—
drives us to link, chain a curtain, thatch a roof; braid vines into electrical cords

Our skirts are shredded into tourniquets; clog arteries resolute on lava, tidal wave—
Rocks crack like pumpkin seeds between our teeth, even in empty mouths.

It's nothing for women who cradle little ones between curtains of incursion—
we have birthed more than one dead son, brother, hostage, girl, flower, stone.

Forts have been built of silk and cement, each hand laying brick upon brick.
The years pass, the beds sag aloneness; graves are hollowed right below the breastbone

We are our own weapons: waiting hardens the calves, teaches us how to move—
          phrases are formed and we mouth ancient stories but nothing

as remarkable as this preservation of life when death lurks. The sergeant asking
questions through the crack in the door our bodies are pressed upon

These days are not remembered, no names are evoked; our shadows slide
          down the wall unnoticed
We are seismic in our keening, this song, a story, told in whispers, starving
                                        ourselves of breath.

Today the sign may be the white flower fallen from the bush
the edges brown, one side wilted or perhaps a child
pointing at the branch arcing like a dragon's neck
quiet breath, wood of fire. We can read drops
streaming the shingles, the condensation on the pane.

Today the sign will be the sound, the sky vibration
jets in the bellies of the clouds or perhaps the song
drifting from the door half-open, hot in a storefront church
at the corner of Macarthur—what we read are sometimes words

or more often the curve of the back, the lines below the eyes
each one explanatory and specific   silhouetting stature
or sickness   one leg gently twisted outward.

Today the sign will be the flutter of Chinese elm leaves,
the comb of the grass to one side, the inversion
of a tree trunk, infested colony in celebration
in soft undersides of ivy, quiet and stretching.

Hear the slap of the oar—the keel humming right beneath
the surface, eggs sunken to bottom.

2

Today the sign will be easy, raked into wheat fields
plucked from dying bean stalks, heard in a note
strayed from the chord chart, stuck to the sole
of the boot.

Today the sign—a matter of course—where you travel or stand.
The rhythm is under breath, below your ear, vibrato
against your windpipe. Each word you utter
is coated by the embryo of a new word
divined from a time untouched and un-designed.

Our skin is under contract
and, in the end, this crisp cloak returns to the earth.
I measure the weight of my granules
feel the shifting toward death along
my neckline crossing my chest looping rib and vertebrate

My heart beats a ripple across the skin
the lungs inflate/deflate softened by fine hairs
and scented oils, nerve fibers violining a restless music down
my legs mounting joints and skiing shins, ankles and feet

I feel its dust—the desert composition, canyon and mesa,
alive and dead at the same time

This dust, infinity sheds its cells, the surface fuses elements:
dermis, pores, corneum—scars a silhouette of bodies gone—
here at the end of my fingertips
shivers a cold anxiousness   reluctant absolution

And what does this make me?
Element upon element, mineral mixed with platelets and papillae—
Am I a mountaintop above tree line pulling my roots toward nourishment
or an arroyo sunk into the abdomen the sedimentary pelvis of the desert?
How do I stir my earth into life?

The town he grew up in is falling into the ocean. He is unmoved by this sinking:
the sea is reclaiming its turf, he says, the surrender is predictable. That building
where his father liberated him too soon sinks into its hips and cracks
an arrow in the stucco pointing to the cloudy always sky   out of sight
he turns his back on it and the beach where he lived cold   out of mind

It's just that easy to let go, you wonder, of home or homeland, of tribe or country
drift on the water between there and here and not look   empty the sand that once
ran through your fingers, gripped and released.
                                        You're not sure half the time where you are—
home is different from homeland. One you hold and one slips away or burns in the
atmospheres, abandoned. Pieces fall in unknown territories and are absorbed into the land.

He studies what's under the earth, not what's on top of it. Listens for the seismic echoes
follows the liquefaction, water floating in, sand siphoning out—a hypertension signaling
the first rumbles, a schism of the crust, the heart breaking, leaving a story behind
that strangers tell each other without pity for the ground below. His stories are
          subterranean—
          the confinement of fire giving way.

In exile we write of lost cities, countries that formed the friction ridges on our fingerprints;
every story pushes harder as if articulation is redemption   or at the very least allows us
to point to the place on the map where the house once stood. Maybe all of that:
houses and schools, roads and churches, even the neighbors are less the point
when the foundation gives way. Everything can be lost just that quick.

His relationship with memory is scant; he numbers the stories that are told
and are so well-rehearsed you wonder if they happened. Like the home
by the sea,
          they sink slowly, not into the ground or into the ocean,
          but into the skin so tough we leave bits everywhere we go.
          We must be aware of the matter below, what skins materialize when lying fallow
                    what conjuring stirs up this earth.
                    Step lightly, keep moving, home is up ahead.

You think these are tears
a cluster of stars weighing lash
and lid but in fact

They are numbers, clicks on the odometer—
miles between where I was and where
I'm going

They glide in and out of sight like an eye
opening and closing and I keep on course

The chimes of the clock and their insistent
time moves forward without doubt

This momentum has nothing to do
with you, only with what's ahead
and how I have to move aside

II. Coming Clean

...you are not accountable
to the life of your tribe
the breath of your planet...
Adrienne Rich, *North American Time*

Stones on the eyes flatten brown light
to dark--a blink shutters the thing we don't mean to see—
yet a constant reminder hangs like a sty in every corner,
flashes blepharospasm: a body lying in the grass
a scar on the child's leg, a writer scratching apparitions.

Rubbing eyes harshly only burns them—
clean the lenses, rinse cool,
blow on the tips for small relief
floaters obscure lashes,
impossible to clear. Rake the eyelid—
the lacrimal nerves sing so the whole body
shudders and eyes fall heavy and still.

Forever the ultimate fear is losing a piece of our mind:
of drawing a blank at the faces of loved ones
and unknow their names or why they have come,
baffled by the repetition, speech insistent slow
enough to bring memory to the foreground.
Here's what to remember:

It's still in our skin. Our veins wash corpuscles
flow sea pebbles into the archive, each canal
collects the moment where she paused
and thought for a minute then couldn't recall.
That moment is suspended, quiet.

This is vital. We reshape like cliff sides
buffering the sea. Take a long look
and recognize the width of hips, yours, hers,
the stance of legs and pronouncement of jaw.
We blister from the countless times we have relived—
year after year. Our bodies are strangers, the skin filo.

Enter at a new point where memory resigns
to shadows and dreams. Data reshapes
to music hums undertones our ears—
Soothe to forget without remorse. Nothing says
we cannot start again without pain,
even when our children feel lost. They
won't hurt again. We can start at any time.

Add nothing to the shattered bird—lone creature
that resisted the sun when the sun
*was the only desert that burned—*Ray Gonzalez

COMING CLEAN

Take back your stories, carts of stones,
tears and glances. Take back the tokens,
yellow papers in languages that do not fade
with age. Keep the words to the songs
you hum when you are alone.
                        Clasp against
your sweater the leaf and its silver back.
Hide the envelope you find empty of the letter
someone else tucked into a pocket.
Line your belt with the gold string that tied
your heavy hair as you were waiting, left behind.

                    There are reasons I have never walked
                    the desert alone open to the air and its
                    grains of memory.

Release the fist that held your belongings
to wool, silk and silver picture frames.
Surrender the courtesies in your own language,
the smile, embrace, kiss on each cheek. Turn in
your name and its complicated consonants
its delicate meaning, its position in the sky.

                    The sun is definite. It beats on my back,
                    scorching my skin with the whip marks
                    of your history.

You are not the only people to come here
toting your secrets in the lines in your hands
in the moons of your fingernails, the lowered
lids of your eyes. You may live head down

for who knows how long, counting the blocks
beneath your feet, the streets to your apartment,
the miles to your country, the stretch of sand
between you and home.

You are safe now. You will learn silence
as you have never known it; privacy
as you have never craved it. You will lose
contact with old friends and not hold
your children responsible for bringing you
tea at two o'clock, or cradling a daughter
who ears are specked gold. Loud conversation
will be hushed, pungent smells eliminated, longing scorned.

                    In this desert
                    we walk without companions
                    or shade. We feed off the sun
                    the only living creature
                    we can rely on.

I have seen you looking across the landscape
trying to find the familiar markers, the touchstones,
the mileage signs that should direct you.
You remember the bend of the river, the opening
in the fence, the two trees that grew together
as if they were embracing. And you remember
the desert, not vast and forbidding, not lonely
or leading to madness. In its warmth, you have sung
a million songs, recited thousands of poems,
embellished all the old stories as if they were yours,
not seeing then, how they floated into the air,
sifted into the wind, sailed away from you,
gathering with other words—refugees to the sun.

*THE PROPER PURGATION**

Peace to a grove of figs.
Peace to this darkness.
Peace to a shell that hid its blood in wet sleep.
Peace to this ruin.

From *Thank You Imru Ul-Qais*
Saadi Yousef, tr. by Khaled Mattawa

Barbed muscles twist names mix wire
with home, home wraps around heart
heart grows a shell in hopes we do not learn
again what is happening and what
is happening to whom, trying to mark one
two to declare our innocence and our absence
our silence is the only way to live some think
you see writhing/writing hurts so much,
the tearing so insistent and monsoons flood in
drown the lobes that move each action
to emotion and if we could only control
eyes and ears, elements that rupture
the skin the boils swelling inside the underarm,
lining the mouth holding the unspeakable
until nothing until the silence leaks
until the temporal levees crash the walls
until a certain construction unravels rebar
plaster shedding the ventricles arteries aorta
bypass grief bypass horror bypass saying
it's unspeakable it is not the proper purgation
rhythm, 'harmony' and song; we are just in time
bypass the humidity of history and its recognizable scars
we inflict repeatedly, inoperable deconstruction
these words are not enough
are not coming as quickly as tragedies do
our language is not our language instead
invented by the murder of the heart,
of hearts ruptured by magnitude coming
too fast and the words hold fire hanging
in wait and what we want to say is not

that this is our world smothered every moment
a massacre seen as bodies and not brothers
seen as battlefields and not homes
seen as acts of god and not the godless
I reach for the syllables to put together
the artistic ornament that moves us to Act Three
where we say peace peace peace to this ruin.

what can you do but sit and survey the tracks where the ambulance
had stopped yards away from the body and see the flies gather
where the driver was struck by the bullets? the smoke in the air
lingers days old stale sorrow the kind that settles into your throat
can't be coughed out even when singing the old songs that erupt
from the chest the roughest way out the notes as hard as pebbles.

your hangout the café where fuul simmers fresh parsley and scallions
in pots on blue flames throws a shadow on a map of blood
drawn on the sidewalk where **X** his feet are shot and **X** he is hit
in the back and **X** the ambulance arrives and **X** the driver
cannot navigate the storm of fire and fear and **X** the street fills
with mourners a matter of course the words fly rocks and melodies

each body is its own island and the waters gather round splashing
against the shores pushing a million heartbeats against the silence
exhaling a thousand zaghrat pumping into the lungs everything
they have. Children are lost everywhere and their bodies form
land masses a new diagram that must be inset into our geographies
so we know where we stand.

sip tepid water slow now wait again for the beans to cool
the metal of the spoon stains your mouth leaves sulfur
on your tongue. You cannot eat here
                    anymore   and you cannot leave.

ASCENSION

What do exiles do but continue to walk
in countries where they were not born?

And when they leave are their ghosts alone,
wandering routes river to home to horizon?

Breath visible from the cold of death
I call you to smoke and vapor

———

We search for the lost through shards of cement
a crusty coffee cup impossible to read.

The cities are homes as much as they are tombs
you draw the map, a longitude of loss

The names of the storytellers will be catalogued
next to saints, teachers, revolutionaries, and bread makers

———

How many times can your heart break?
How many ways is writing a surgery?

Mahmud, it is too much to hold
I stand in the square and call for you

You pierce the voices of this city—
the sky over Ramallah is refrain

Because You Create Amazing Things

for Tony Khalife

...the uncommon language is where truth is holding up
speaks itself into obscurity and only a few reach down
to letters at the bottom of trunk, paper laced antique—
covets the secrets told behind spotted hands, tucked into the pockets
of the younger ones, who sometimes forget to retrieve them
until we are searching for ourselves

...a letter came today and you say now, I know the story
the details come in thirty-eight words of the so—called common language
and we know what it means without interpretation.

You are angry—
not at the horror but at the hiding—at the words swallowed
through a scratchy throat that will not heal—chafed from the reflex
of holding them down.

This will never make history: the ugliness of men, the violations,
the death of love, postponed—until the last lie is incinerated.

Swallow her legacy, forgive her brutality and her silence.
We speak in tongues that rise like heat, scatter the ashes
of a dead past. Ours is the language of invisible ink.

Everything you touch is dusted with the remnants of her words—
you can see generations of fingerprints on your guitar and tabla.
As you recite it aloud, write it in this letter, retell it over, you know—
all language is unreliable, temporary, prone to misunderstanding.
Truth was there all along and wrote your story to a tee.
Honor it. Honor her.

RE: My Father's House is a Terrorist Target

for Hayan Charara

1.

The subject line of an email
The subject line of the phone call
The subject line of my shortness of breath

      My father—in high dry grass in Maryland
      stands in the sun and lifts his head listening for danger

Your father slows his car on the highway heading
toward Beirut, a few miles ahead, tea and anise
cookies in a cupboard; a few miles south,
the beds are empty, the sofa losing the impression
of his body.

      My father drifts on the path, leaves
      the television talking behind him loud enough
      the neighbors hear what he doesn't,
      the phone rings sorrowful notes
      children asking about home, his brothers—
      twists buttons off his shirt counting them
      like pennies and the years he left Lebanon behind

Your father takes his other son and wife home,
slows his car to see the damage, flare up the pupils burn
breath held back: It is routine to turn around, to hope
for Beirut—

      My father alone in the yard implores
      his mother and my mother
      as the fireflies rise up and orbit
      around his head—knows that he cannot return

2.

We both sit at the other ends of lines
our arms covering our heads, a kind of prayer
and protection from memory and anger
and shortness of breath.

In all of this, you are not the son sitting
in the back of the car reaching a hand forward
as the city burns.

> I am not the daughter pulling my father back
> into the house as he whispers the air

You write the subject line:
my father's house is a terrorist target
and I want to answer each word of that line
breathe deep into the dust and disaster, but cannot—

I slow down a few miles away, gaze outside the glass
and find myself stuck. I cannot move beyond *my father's house…*

for Suheir Hammad

A child named Jenin—
comes into a half-world
hollowed and hardened
hands flattened, pushing
boulder upon boulder
mistaking grief for strength.

She knows this is the time of silence,
bones tossed under the skin,
knotting together histories: arms and legs,
necks tattooed with others' names.

Jenin cannot unearth the dead, return the poet to the line interrupted
she does not call upon shadows to stand in light, to sit at the table
clutching or to scatter the birds away from bodies.

nothing
is remembered without plowing incantations crushed beneath the shattered city.

Here is your world, Jenin,
you are baptized with limestone
and sand, thorns grow between rocks
entwine your fingers so raw
they cannot unweave sorrow.

We are here now.
Sit. Sit at the table,
take the tea, hold the glass warm against
your palms.

You follow Fuad, the young son
He shows his room a drawing he has made of a horse
on his walls: unicorns and dinosaurs.
You touch his shoulder, stroke his hair—tell him
you are not afraid of extinction
you want to cover his eyes
not have him look toward the sea flattened by metal swollen smoke.

In the mosque you admire the arches inlaid
lapis and ivory, sheen of water. Follow the carpets long
runners of miracles in thread.   Spines of men curl
into echoes of the muezzin. You want to worship like them,
the quiet echo of prayer filling the cage of your chest.

2.

We are waiting, what do we do in the face
of these bombings? Do we gather our jewelry and books?
Do we send our children across the border
to live in refugee camps?
What do we pack?   The coffee urn
father brought from turkey? The pair of earrings
specially chosen for the wedding day?
What will become of the tick on the wall
marking the children's growth?
The groan of the washing machine?
The bare spot on the rug where Jiddi put his feet
when he read the Friday paper?

3.

Fear is an uprising rattling against the incarceration of will—
time to leave
        you think   the history writes you out
of this ruined civilization you don't know
except for the wine-colored thread woven in your hair
the shard of cobalt needle to awakening
and the chambers of hearts weakening.

The needs are basic:
Rose wood chests and cedar cupboards
chairs with red velvet seats. Was that their house?

      Or a house leveled
      or assumed or stolen or sold?

      The plain stone one with pictures
      taped against green peeling walls—
      a favorite poet, revolutionary leader, singers from America.

When they were moved in, little thought
was given to the table   where the chickpeas
ground the pestle so hard on her shoulders
she rolled them loose while dressing, rubbed down the shrug.

No notice was given to the shelves
where the Quran sat, worn leather
soft as hands, covered with her mother's black scarf

      Crates held 7-Up bottles that they wished filled with milk.

Most food came in packages: they threw away
wrappers, not stems, leaves or seeds.

Someone talked about painting the cabinets that stored
dried mint in old tahini jars, sandy crackers
in green and white cardboard, fava beans in yellow cans.

Beds were few, fit the young ones together
according to size. Hoped they never grew
took to the streets, marched.
      They listened for their familiar whispers in the dark.

II

Clothes were shaken out, sprinkled
with water seeping between her fingers,
pressed while she thought   outside traffic
      clogged the dusty streets—smoke heavy and hanging
      on mustaches of the old men
      who sighed at the boys shooting fingers at each other.

Then chairs were brought out, arranged in lines to seat the elders
who arrived early for Hassan and Nerma's wedding.

Two borrowed arms covered with white sheets
the bride and groom sit at the crest of the circle.

From these chairs, drums beat and flute echoed
not crackling, no radio, no bullets, no bottles brewed with fire.

In these chairs, they sang, clapped for the dancers
and touched each other's fingers in stillness.

Someone hit a teacup with a spoon
a bell of invitation.

III

3 days and raptors poured smoke, fire breathed
in the underbelly, unloading missiles, gumball quick
then Hassan looked up and then ran—
      the scalpel ripped across the ground
      and five policemen gone to dust and cinders.

IV

White sheets unravel to cover the faces
Hassan is lifted where Nerma's face hung
over his the night before   just the night before

Line up the chairs in a solid line
put the elders in front. The seats damp and soft
from the wedding are brushed by a mother's hand.

Count the chairs, the way they count
candles on birthday cakes, the number of children
in each family, years lived in a house

the grades finished in school, months
of a pregnancy, pages of a book, the endurance
of a war, anniversaries.

They count the chairs
    lined up for the funeral. Nerma listens deeply
        numbers the ribs, the vertebrae, the bones

    her tightened cheeks.   She counts the tiny gasps in her heart
            Mourners march—she counts
            only their feet and how long it takes

                to pass from the first chair to the second to the third
                and then to the cradle of her husband swaddled
                        to be given.

I fail to distinguish what is solid and what is liquid—
rock hard is not reliable, the wind cannot diminish
an already dying face   at the broken window
errant meteors   a surge of rockets collapse the sky

I pray with my cheek to the ground my god
seeps into the pores shrouded hand and temple
forehead marked as I am marked undeniable
allegiance to the foundation on which I stand

children do not sleep   do not play without fight—
avert our gaze from what is missing   fragment
adrift in rock boulder knobs shards of glass
nothing more surrounds me each of us open sea

we make bargains with the heavens to stop
            voice my whisper   rise up my story: include the name
            of this land as the home of my father, this country
            inherit my children and it would never be undone,
we swallow the earth closer to our own death

Our garden bordered an alley which crossed into a hayfield and stretched to the hillside
Our yard had lilacs that surrounded a pond filled with sweat peas and crested by vines
Our porch led to a street that lined the road running from our house
all the way to West Virginia and we walked from one house to Neff woods
     from another to the waterfall across a bridge

The coalmining corner of Pennsylvania with all its faults let cows chew from this neighbor
    to the next and children crossed yards that were not theirs
    to get to school and sit on the steps of someone's porch
    without asking and we didn't know that this was belonging

This was Pennsylvania and not Abu Dis where a wall was erected right down main street
keeping the kids away from the school they've been going to their whole lives—so what
do they do? they wonder, like the farmers of Azzoun whose vegetable fields, olive trees

are out of reach, who stare at the twenty five feet of stone and wire, guarding them
from their own food as a security measure that forces a four-kilometer walk
    to get in a gate that gives them twenty minutes to slip over
    to the other side for bushels of barley

to take home, if it's still there or if you live in Ana'ta district in East Jerusalem,
it's probably not—some things had to move to make room for the wall and
    without your home everyone is more secure.
    The landscape is sliced and lands are carved and contained.

I have studied maps—the blue waters and the green mountains, yellow countries
and red ones all meant something to the cartographers and I followed them,
a puzzle of colors explained in the legend in the corner that said this was the earth:

Lakes, mountains, cliffs, buttes, highways, hiking trails, one way streets, capitols, borders
mileage counters, oceans, river snaking through states and countries, ranges peaking
across the Urals, frozen tundra, pampas, veldt, thickly populated cities, railroad tracks

I run my finger along each symbol, each road designation, each color, each touchstone
How do you mark a barrier? Make it part of a landscape? What is the symbol
of restraint? What is the color of confinement, disruption, loss and
separation? Of sorrow? How do you hold that pen, diagram the atlas, sketch the captivity?

          Do not draw the wall of the Great March to liberation,
          just mark a slow death to the earth that inhabits
          it and the people who make it home.

I want the mothers to sign contracts
that they will take their secrets with them—
they won't unearth the relics of children gone
or lose the imprint of their thumb on the knob
of the stove in a house left long ago.

I want them to hide inside prayers that hum
the house in darkness and hold the silence that makes
singing a miracle. Don't speak the old language, courted
by melodies and incantations. Abandon the commandments
that have ruled so long. Secure the drawer holding pillow cases
filled with letters.

Mothers have no debt on this earth, everything is paid off.
I know who I am without the dissembling of the DNA,
the counting of fibers and cells and comparisons
of form and skin color. Don't use my eyes to reminisce.
Don't forget where you are and talk to old friends
who haven't been seen in forty years.
They are not here; I am.

Mothers, you can go. Hard as it is to keep the trunk packed tight
lode into infinity. Carry it off to wherever is afterwards.
Or forget about it all together. As much as we whisper to you,
we really can't hold all that is there. Don't remind us that the dying
have no regrets. Nothing can be done. Sorrow can be felt only
by the living.

for Donna Wolf

At the Friends Meeting House
Fourth and Arch, Philadelphia

                   we stood Arab and Jew
                   poetry
                   lying flat on a podium

the wooden benches crossed the room like musical lines
dotted with notes: flat, sharp, minor chord and natural

we began
our hymns   Zimerot & Nashid

histories
convictions
invocations

                   Eppur si muove

—

         Something in the air
was pollinating, a quick silent
buzzing, an unforgettable murmur

a crack of light a door widened,
flattened open and barrowed in two
police summoned for the idea

           of us two   in embroidered blouses
                        and fringed shawls and a fissure
        in the hearts where the poems were
        created, willing to show them to
                 others and ourselves.

We stopped, waited, while
the director hustled them away
        as if the electricity had gone out
        an emergency that would be taken
        care of. A clear room that had lost

its innocence in the one brief moment
one momentary violation. Hushed
by candlelight   the energy of sorrow
was bigger.

III. I Make Nothing But Words

> …Everything is real.
> I knew I was casting myself aside . . .
> and flew. I shall become what I will
> in the final sphere..
> Mahmoud Darwish, *Mural*
> Tr. Sargon Boulus

IN THE THROAT I

if I could speak
the hyphen making space between the word and what it needs

then I could learn how this body can inhabit two worlds—a cable surging
power from one land to the next

I could verbalize
a delicacy of reference, elbow the comma to clarify, that I am not recent
but a long time resident holding a steady job, not belonging to unworthy society

Simplified
by the colon that factualizes my history to be concurrent with yours
despite my name that could be translated, not to the same tongue

Perhaps explain
that many things are true; that I am connected without conjunction
and the woman with my face died with all our names woven under her hair.

1. Speech is not an Act or even a formality,
    no reduction, denotation/ inference or entendre;
    it rustles the fine needles at the tops of the trees,
    closer to where air thins, and we starve
    to speak, gasp before we breathe.

2. When I listen, language abrades the line,
    violates the memory of how
    it was dreamed/ imagined,
    sold to the rebelling citizens. They tattooed
    their arms with petroglyphs of seasons.

3. The syntax of history cracks at the seams:
    the clauses, major and minor, sometimes
    switch place: voice and silence, privacy and suspicion.
    Words are stolen, words repeat, slandering their past.

4. In the diagram of these sentences the modifiers
    are thorns; the nouns, thistle, making poetry
    near impossible/ instruments are in the wrong hands—
    Carve the message into the bark,
    a trail map in many tongues

5. The original intention less important
    than the best intention, the sleight of hand
    shifts nominative and object. We cannot know
    if it's shadow or element.

6. Some are born so late they have no questions.
    The ferns are slide rules, the petals compasses.
    They must get dirty to listen—every word,
    every word holds history and meaning-
    and denies all.

7. You can arrange and rearrange, acid-rain
            the foliage to discoloration fertile/futile
            Remember to speak the words faithfully,
            expose the translation, unmask discourse,
            placement of properties and utterances.
            This is a time for clarity:

If I speak from the heart my
words have bloodflow, they harbor in the atrium, meditate quietly
      rattle, mix with cloistered virtues, oxygen-rich
      travel through chambers drip from the vessel
                  to the brain—
      our truest words siphon the blood that rushes
      upward, thumps behind the temples
      the stones unearthed from the cold wattage of
      lonesomeness, the ebb and flow—compassed by
      the hollow of the clavicle, collarbone, and throat.

If I speak from the gut, an intestinal patois gushes
a story marked by decisions and bits of anguish
ingested on the fly, something unsure, nourished with
smoked chickpeas, yerba mate, half moons of pears
      unrecognizable but elemental, organic, light on salt.

      I dream up stews of poems from the lower bowels
      and acid-tinged stories that burn their way
      through the esophagus, a film on the tongue.
            Words lost in the interior pathways, snarling in and out
            of salvage and debris—it's cleaning up after the party
            and they are satisfied though humbled by the neighborhood.

Arteries sometimes collapse, diaphragms distend, an
indigestion of thought and I am speechless. The rumble
in my body doesn't generate syllables or sense. And the quiet
is a hunger, a palpitation, pressure dropping and veins
stringy and unsure.
      I look for these breaches, the pebbles chime
      inside the shell, disturb the biology of inception.
      My fibers knit to harden, to extend the vocal chords the
      body goes to quiet, to reason, to mind, and I am lost
            tapping into each organ-divining.

I Make Nothing But Words

These years are in suspension—hammer
      thinking of the parts
      under-utilized, not sleeping
      or meditating—off production,
pound down the hours that could
mean so much more

in the middle between explosion
and dexterity, there is no progression
only the decomposition of energy
and atrophy of fiber and the knitting
of hemp, afraid to lift a finger too late

Someone is missing here and the search
is still on—not
      the teacher, more the storyteller
      behind the activist hides alchemist
      the prophet slips coins to the weaver

This is not an industry; I am making nothing
but words
      in and out creeping
      past margins, sliding off borders
      calculated into smudges
that patch fissures in the surface
of lives that bump against my skin.

FOREHEAD

Sometimes I'm afraid to look
to see how far the lines reach
forked from temple to temple

Lines that are not barred but open
leaving space for notes drawn haphazardly
We are treble clef as much as we are
accidentals; sharp, flat and natural.

Still I resist, mother, to own the etching
you scratched on my forehead with doubt
and derision. I have grown into them
reluctant to hear it with maestoso

I am rutted with your history, my forehead
the symphony of lonely travel, of ripping
rags between my teeth, moving vivace
eyes fixed so as not to dream to not remember

the song that would lay chords on our brow—
room for the rich full notes, the bass staff
mumbling under your breath—molto ritenuto
the life you didn't have.

When they are deeply carved, I'm asked
if I am tired, if my day is sorrow. There is something
between us, they don't know, ummi
I carry your lines, the notes, the staff, the beats
rewriting your song, note by note, from temple
to temple, written on my face, an octave higher
your voice my metronome.

Poets are dying and I am
of an age where we shared
conversations lifted from keys
      that were hard-tapped, hit
      fingertip callus.

      Paper, not screen, struck
      pecked pressed lines with carbons
      palms of poetry each sheet
      the words lighter fading
      faster, pressed into my hand
      a mirror image of poem.

Poets who were the first
of their kind, names stuck in teeth,
introduced with clumsy pronunciations
dropped out, snuck off as expected
before the museum of natural
history could display their skeletons
in glass-enclosed dioramas, seat them
at wooden desks their boney feet
covered with shoes I know they
would not wear; ashtrays
overflow with Styrofoam
cigarettes, crushed.

These old ramblers, parted out
a good radiator and gearbox
voice on an audio clip
a performance uploaded to You-
Tube musicians louder than words
the mouth moves ghost syllables
the writer vibrates.

We knew something
reeked of that life spoiled rotted
at the bottom of a mason jar
algae-covered. The page was
silent almost unnoticed.

Readings had been solemn events—
we sat like footlights anticipating
the cry or shout or tear down.
We depended on those poems
for vengeance.

Cork bits floating in wine bottles
fingertips creeping
toward the others who we
would slip away with in sympathy.

Poets are dying—their filet cuts
distributed to anthologies always
featured toward the later pages—one
of each. Retrospectives minor gatherings hummed
vespers while journals went out of print
weeks after publication.

The complete works require
archeology, labeling of the bones
sorting femur from tendon, ligament
sinew, using the old guides, anatomy
frayed at the edges, translucent pages—
the new technology then.

Omitted the DNA smeared on the finger
strengthened from a life of hand-
drawing the architecture of language
and then letting it go.

The poets are dying I am
right behind them—my case
has a hard side worn on the bottom,
secured with rope and labeled—to protect
the words gathered by light, etched
in the air.

This age stretched
my hand from pen to particle
to pixels, silence and alleys
to coffee and microphones. We make
adjustments because we cannot stop. Now
in these later years, the light comes toward
us. We can write in the dark.

HOLE

Over the last week three lenses
dropped out of my glasses

I found them like seashells
washed up on my coffee table
on the seat of my car
under my shoe

they were irreparable
refused to fit back into the frame
of one pair of glasses for reading
or the other against the sun
or the third light against the dark

perhaps my eyes were not meant
to have them after all liberating
one eye to its own strength/
weakness might not be a mistake

like on that sunny day
the two views of the sky
squinted and cracked into shards
shaded and glossy, a surgical
reinterpretation of the horizon

or when I read, one eye
gleaning the words defined
in their own articulation, the
other chasing language
giving in to its ambiguity

those nighttime lenses, ones
that singularized double images
in the dark, now missing one
side too and the moon shifts

                         from one eye
two now one, two now one—
the movie screen has a light
shredded fringe and the characters
a desired complexity.

I can accept these openings,
toss away the shaped glass
shaded, magnetized and ground.
Something has to be left
for me to see for myself—
the world, the way
I was meant to find it.

Neck

Two years ago my throat was cut
a tender slice opening the cavern
where poison had holed up and hung
like mussels attached to rocks
feeding on the plankton of my thyroid.

The removal was quick   the line
almost invisible, nothing lingering
        no complaint   more
        room to swallow, a wider berth
        of breathslide trombone.

A simple scar   it falls
in the creases of my neck
wraps a wire around my voice
        stuffs my breath into my chest
        restricts the current of language—

this thorny interior where words dangle
precipitously perched at the tunnel
        a waiting station studying a dicey triptych:
           bowels   womb
      heart
lungs   windpipe   throat   neck
        radioactivity detected

My voice harbors me   assembles angry
cells jammed in center lane pileup

the executioner's knife was tender
recognized my innocence   slipped a blade
into aging skin and left undetected.

Still and all I clear my throat
hang amulets and mandalas   open
for candlemas beeswax crossed above the clavicle.
          Something is there   undetected
          fevering the trachea   flaming the larynx
          I swallow   I swallow with ease
speak with delicacy.

for Anthony

We cannot divulge secrets for there are none—
no formula, format or sense of organization.
Our conversations are ordinary in the way of
keeping a house secure, a life safe. We gather at the table
and sometimes talk, sometimes don't, glancing occasionally
at the dirtied napkin or the fragmented plate.
It's a love story that rode the river like a branch floating—
jamming in the corners, freeing, and moving again.

We were buoyant, landed softly and we accepted
the impulse, no longer impulsive, a matter of consequence.
This is not to say we don't gather fire, find it in the moments
of shadow when I turn to you on a flight across the world
and you're not there. But misery is not the secret either.
I can walk you anywhere I go and know you buy the warm cashews,
talk animatedly to the juice vendor who does not understand you
but learns your name.

This is the pulse for me. The way peace washes the inside of my mouth
tempering the fury, disarming the aftershock of memory which could have led
away but didn't. I could live your life a little just the way you do and you can
live mine, without having studied me. Take my word, not just my body,
take the belief in this and the hard hitch to the post just outside your door.
Any thing more would destroy me than the ordinariness of this—
nothing more lustrous can reveal the course.

On Christmas day, my father teaches his granddaughter
to crack walnuts with her bare hands. He gathers two in his fist
their bark scraping against his palm. His fingers are long
and old country elegant, bronze, manicured and strong.
When he flexes his palm, the nuts divide, opening
cleanly as lemons, the flesh intact in the heart.

His granddaughter cannot believe she can do this,
hands so small, loose as cattails. Use both
he prompts, meaning her hands and chooses
two walnuts for her, almost identical in size. She clasps
her fingers together and presses, her shoulders rise,
her neck stretches, the veins on the back of her hand
fill with blood.

Her palms, open, blush with failure, the two nuts rolling
against each other. My father reaches over and turns them,
tells her, try again. He nods confident, flicks a finger forward.
She is that kind of girl, one who holds worlds inside her hands,
one who will push. When the nuts meet, this time, everything
gives in—their crack is scientific, the dissection, a neat surgery.

They lie open on the coffee table, unwhole, yet not broken.
My father picks out the meat, it doesn't take strength, he says.
He draws a circle around them, where the two halves come
together, it's where they are weak. Position them
at their points of vulnerability.

His granddaughter rejoices, runs to show her brother
her new trick. I take one walnut, rattled it beside my ear,
I have been deceived by the stubbornness of the shell,
the strength of the construction, stronger than teeth.

We crushed them with rocks and hammers, lining them up
on the porch after they fell from the tree, shed
their green crisp coat, ready to be eaten. They did not
split as they gave way to our instruments, exposing
the compartments of their interior. Crushing mixed
the inside and the outside into heaps of crumbs.

We were scavengers, picking out flesh from bone,
satisfied with getting in anyway we could.

Is it too much to say there is finer humanity
in breaking walnuts by hand? Is it too false
to find lines of connection, seams of conjunction,
and push against them ever so slightly without the sloppiness
of destruction or residue of incompetence?
The simplicity of this is trustworthy- too classical to borrow from.

I think of the forces I can push with my hands:
silence against loneliness, peace against pity,
the tremble of love against whispers at dusk.
So much is offered to us that simultaneously erupts
as we touch it ever so gently.

First there is wonder
Sun like a god directs
the breathing the color
of face, the page of skin

Fold in grace two pair
the ancients there are
women hearts hammered
metal and love wasted
on kings/pharaohs

A jar of memory
scrape the bottom
of my tongue for unused
words, Arabic childhood
dreams and curses

Music, dance, loud

hands wide clapping
the smile is in the eyes
when the whole room
oud and drum

Patience quiet desert
not of the people I hold
back not remember when
others are held down
can't blame anyone but
my own country

A brand new hope
washed the old one
starched the color
and placed neatly on top
waiting for an open border

Old religions books medals
from the chains around
my neck hangs my name
pagan hieroglyphics,
Arabic scroll, cross missing

perhaps in pockets of jeans
inside: shoes, notebooks and toiletries
pile the whispers of ummi
in the market, baba
with the pipe

Unfinished writing scrawled
journals badly written
wait for sand in the pen
carved in rocks, shapes
of the past transported
My heart signatured to country

FIRST THE MORNING CUP OF COFFEE.

I asked for the blend as I remember my dad does—
one-quarter blonde, the rest dark, and lots of cardamom (Suheir Hammad)

Coffee beans have wisdom
so fierce mouths fill
with smoke and knowledge
with extra sugar memory
sweetens and morning
exhumes hope from fear
milk bursts dandelion
puffs the scent is unforgiving
and forgotten
small cups silken the lips
mugs strengthen the hands

In Egypt the pot is watched
until the face rises to the surface
and then it is ready
For us, you boil, grounds
swirling a whirlwind madness
three times until surrender

Cardamom remembers walks
across white mountains, hickory
scents dark waters on the gulf shore

Our inheritance is this fragrance
fingertips distinct and tangy
and the chime, stirring this song
each day.

BIRTHDAY

When he turns one hundred next year we will celebrate
that he continues to live without wife job country

Without friends who can speak to him like his brothers
in the old language that he diluted like roubeh

into the milk of English the big jug from Giant hoping
the laban will taste the same texture smooth but

never does. We will celebrate the strength of his legs
go up and down those stairs twenty times each day

the muscularity of his back and shoulders
his reach up to the high shelf to get the good coffee

when we come to visit show us a picture
he forgot he had hoping we

are titillated by the story he will start then and there
because it's something he knows. We love the stories

the old people can tell
and he is particularly good.

—

We try to be children to him in our own age
with memories banging in the grey sleeplessness

of morning. We want to be guardians hoping on alert
he will never need that kind of care his body or know

that heart will not become like his hearing faint and unsure, faking it half the time.

We do not understand there are conversations
he will never have again across parallel lines

      absolute familiarity
      referentially intact

—

His memory is not going—they think the old
ones cannot remember. But he remembers it all.

He has lived with longing and with silence and no
pity given or received. His ear tilts toward the singing

in church, the phone calls in regular intervals and we
are happy to hear his voice, imagine him at the desk

shouting into the phone with big buttons and a list
of our numbers beside it. We crank out the Arabic

try baba to enunciate it in the jabali way
to take to your country if only for one call.

We are the ghosts in his dull ears reminding him
he is alive and not lost, our life these 100 years.

THAT ISN'T FAITH, THIS IS

for John Herman

You listen
more attentive than most
take mental notes
of where the knife
will enter your chest
where the underground
routes to your heart
have.jammed
and need a bull
dozer to clear the way
replace the cables
resurge the flow

and you retell
it all like a good story
you heard maybe
from the person
sitting next to you
on the plane with
pictures, arrows
and instructions

and I find it funny
that of all the ideologies
that move through
our lives, the gods
false and divine,
the mantras and rosaries
the litanies and songs
the literatures and dogmas
we pray for that knife
to hit right

to not stray, for
the steadiness

of the hand that slips
a vessel from your
leg into your chest
that connects the tubes
like a master pipefitter
it's a lot to expect

from someone and not
god who you may or may
not believe in, someone
who learns your name
ever so briefly, doesn't
know what your heart
means and to whom.

I call it faith, letting
yourself sleep surrounded
by people you don't know
giving your body to
their hands, exposing
the contents of your
heart the way you have
to so few or so many

and I hope that
your heart in their hands
knows a kindness
that strangers give
to one another in brave
circumstances: floods
births, confusion
and fear. This is all
we can believe. That
you may return
refueled and cloudless
love replaced with love
a heart come stronger.

As if marking time prompts the
        bargaining of a life into a
comprehensive accounting, organizing, stitching, storying

Digging up an
        excavation where each bone is examined and
                the heart beat questioned, allowing
forensics to simulate/stimulate the memories,
gorge on the details, events dripping from the mouth,
        wiping relationships
        from the gums
hard to swallow.

I have noted my days more than most,
jived history, cajoled memory, counted
        kin, one after another, none so famous, none so infamous
leaving me to assemble a gathering, a late night argument, and unrepentant decision.

More than this I have indulged in testimony
not heard nor witnessed as *if it were yesterday*
or ever. Life in retelling becomes madness, a
perfect exhibition of the pathology of memory and its insistence.

Queasy at the notion that facts will be tied to me
roped onto my name
        suggesting this life cannot
transform from one day to the next, my name will always be my name, known
unknown
verifiable, counterfeit.

What I prefer is a life anonymous fixed so that
X holds to no photograph, no document, no recording
yielding no memory but the imagined, the unimaginable and in the white space
zero--the images come and go, in and out of the water,
        Face, no face, name, no name, begin again, begin again, begin.

About the Author

Elmaz Abinader is author of a memoir, *The Children of the Roojme: A Family's Journey from Lebanon*, a poetry collection, *In the Country of My Dreams*. She has written and performed several one-women plays: *Country of Origin, Ramadan Moon, 32 Mohammeds, Voices from the Siege* and *The Torture Quartet*. Winner of a Goldies in Literature, a PEN/Josephine Miles Award, Elmaz has been a Fulbright Scholar and the winner of the Oregon Drammies for Country of Origin. She teaches at Mills College in Oakland, and is co-founder of VONA/Voices.